Respect this request, as this is not a wealthy individual, who has spent a great deal of effort constructing her floating thoughts

into concrete words; it has only been through a tremendous level of difficulty and creative prowess she has been able to proceed with this collection of deeply personal, gut wrenching art.

Katalina Rosemond Rourke, Inc. in affiliation with Mila Riportella.

Instagram: @themonalisawassmirking
First Edition: July 2022
This is a self published work done by Katalina Rosemond Rourke, Inc.

The publisher is not responsible for websites (or their content) that are not owned by the publisher.

To find out more, go to the description

Print book interior design by Katalina Rourke.

I would love for you to write In the empty spaces and make them of use.

gaily colored beachball of
rapture.

I was hiding in the false back of a
deep shelf in the library.
with my friend the beachball of
rapture.
hiding and a stark raving mob
marched through chanting my
name
                exhilarating   scary
so my friend seems to have steered
me wrong

but i heard mistakes grant you
knowledge,

so grateful for you gaily colored
beachball of rapture

when i spin you at the beach, you
reflect like a discoball
One eye ensconced in smoke
One eye blinded by fire

beach volleyball
with a plastic inflatable
multicolored beachball

stuck in burning nevada with the
self proclaimed desert trash

Aggression from a sweet place is
overwhelming

Be my friend, I'm very
complementary

i'm aggressive, but it comes from a
sweet place
don't leave me

My chimes of heaven are tiny
bullet ice sloshing around in herbal
tea

Entities shall not be multiplied
without necessity

And my heart sings when I read,

Kissing my doting puppies;

I tap my bum lightly as i pass the
mirror
It's just something i do
Everything's going to be alright
Be cool

Tell them the wooden stake hidden
behind my back was meant to
protect us from the vampires.
gaily colored beachball of rapture

It all sounds more poetic coming
from you
It should have been from you.

the crazy, lovely things girls do.

i think flowers are stupid
useful for the ecosystem but as
decoration- stupid

but felt so special when Chloe gave
them to me after the community
play
and cheering me on when i got my
GED- i was too embarrassed to tell
anybody else
i protest too much about not
needing a friend
i miss her terribly
but i just can't just recreate her
within Martin

Martin is a dunce and it scares me
how he did a swift 360 turn around
from obsessed with Jen to saying
she looked like a man
and how he would fancy bashing
her skull in

and i can't do weird shit with
Martin, like spank wars at work
with the lifeguard paddles on our
breaks.
that was so fucking strange Chloe.
i love that you were always so
strange.

or pulling our shirts down in front
of the mirror and comparing our
boobs:
essentially fishing for compliments

unpopular opinion but i love that
we as girls do that- put ourselves
down just to reassure one another
with beautiful comments.

or jumping and singing into
hairbrushes to the Mamma Mia
musical soundtrack
the unsophistication
the innocence
the ultra girlie things that i suspect
every girl secretly likes to do

or prefacing phone conversations
with an exaggerated valley girl
voice, saying, "this is going to
sound mean…"
like either of us cared

before shredding a professor or
your weird evangelist father who
doesn't believe in christmas,
washing his flea riddled kittens, or
paying a cent of your tuition

or entertaining ourselves by being
convinced your boyfriend was
cheating because the tarot cards
told us so- it was so obvious. even
though we had zero tangible
evidence.
it wasn't funny - it was supposed
to be serious - still we couldn't stop
giggling

or lying to each other about how
angelic we look trying on
unflattering clothes at the mall.

well not so much a lie but heavily
biased, absent of objectivity.
i remember i was a stuffed sausage
in that blouse,
promising each other we looked
like beauty queens
unpopular opinion - but i love that
we can lie and mean it.

the crazy bonding girls do
that only we get
and i miss you

Circling Chains.

time is only a mechanism for
karma

When you evolve the Kara
dissolves

echo cycle is for tigers to eat meat
and cows to chew on grass

the dharma of art is to manifest
beauty
it's not art if it's not beautiful
it can be pretty, it doesn't have to
be
but if it's not beautiful- it's nothing

Bedrocks Of Beauty.

Countenance Of Beauty.
i realised that beauty is the bedrock
of all
not in the way you might suppose i
mean
Life looks of a pastel sunset
But feels of the cool breeze
emanating from the moon

proud in a way that often felt like
quiet rage

the observer is the raw
consciousness itself

the hindu monk setup at the corner
booth of the tattoo convention on
the 17th of May
really saved me
i can directly connect my life
starting to when i read the first
book out of the stack he'd piled on
with no monetary expectation -
that always baffled me.

Jose Guapo from Ep. 18.

My friend selvin told me
on a bridge last June
that i looked like the mona Lisa .
It took me four days ,
But I realised it was the nicest thing
anyone's ever said to me
genuinely.

Jason Momoa always appears in
my dreams with a crow on his
right shoulder.
The harbinger of bad news.
Ik i should take him more
seriously.

Looking menacing w black eyeliner
in a way that feels like he might
burst into song like a Broadway
villain.

don't get how ppl don't get why
ppl feel the need to catfish
since it's so much damn work
it seems almost forgivable to me
And i love
the way they love
Like they're compensating for
something

I love it when ppl hate each other
it's so theatrical
i think bc of the ferocity
(ferocious exchange of energy)

That guy from EP. 18- pretending
to be Jose guapo
Moved
in a way
that was so
fucking funny.

grenadine flavored
quarantine - it feels just like
a movie.

cinnamon cloves,
grated down & sprinkled into
chilli.

skyline's blue then green when
your eyes keep giving.
zoom lecture halls buffering-

what on Earth is he talking
about?

rainbows distorted like peyote trip
torture.

striking and it's completely
dizzying.

half a dozen sommer salts
just barely stick the landing

Hot Summer Day
nervous stomach-
bubbling up throw up.

slushies and sticky nights
 with fireflies.

dogs just won't stay in the fence.

it's so much fun watching dvds
when the internet's out- it's so
quiet
but it feels, i guess just like a
movie.

Ain't Life a Scream.

As i melt in Dr teal's Epsom salt
soaking solution in the bathtub
with a ring around it bc my legs
shook too much to clean

Ain't Life A Scream.

My glutes imbalance is killing me
as I lay binging catfish in bed
lazin in the sunny afternoon,
that show is anything you could
ever need.

And i should rrly worry more
about the "emf rays"

electromagnetic frequency
emitting from my technology.
And the bombs shooting off in
 Somalia,
 Ukraine,
 and Palestine.

I have the time
Just not the bandwidth

Ain't life a scream

Anytime somebody compliments
someone on tv i squeal like it's for
me
I scream.

As i think longly ab which goddess
to worship, which one will grant
me the most beauty
Criss Cross in the swinging chair
attached to the front yard tree

The children are walking home
from school
and it's the only time I feel safe in
this neighborhood

A truck wizzes by
and screams white power outside a
police training facility
that shares a building with the at
risk community center across the
street

Scratch that- it's still not safe

But isn't life a scream

---

omega.

Girl in pieces
Walks with Jesus
The wind u blew
Flew me to my knees
In the flowered grass-
Where the bees lick.

psi.

Acclaim is this all consuming thing
 It eats u and it eats others too

 It eats u but first it gets u fat
by plating up people for u to
consume
and then bye bye all of u.

I just want for money
So i can lie and watch tv
And write short movies.
And eat things that are sweet.

omega (v2).

Girl in pieces
Walks with Jesus
The rain u spit
Flew me to my knees
In the muddy grass-
Where my veins itch.

chi.

my preference is kettle corn
but the sweets were killing me
so i've switched to buttered
now it's clogging my arteries.

phi.

i did talk shows to the mirror every
morning
i've never found a mirror i didn't
love
and what i see could fill a book
i like when things don't make any
sense.
i didn't feel good just then,
aren't lawyers supposed to get you
off?

upsilon.

pink flames

pretty designs on my mother's bic

lighter growing up

made me feel

like the fire that starts

 when your thumb sparks the

wheel

and gets a slight rug burn.

gums in the rain im sorry.

the smell after the rain
all my sisters are full of shit

fanta smoothies

bubblicious cherry cola
bubblegum

radioactive cherrybomb

my hopes and dreams
 u and me.

i can see u in my dreams anymore

i remember feeling alive

how to steal the world.

real life
desires within young girls

i go to the beach in my mind just to
see u.
i like the sand fine but as the world
turns
wasting time with u has been the
biggest
joy of my whole life.

golden lines kiss the skin
being with u feels better than the
rush i
get from peeling my lips off.

dance workout on the strip with
80s malibu barbie

shine bright

i hate john hughes movies *im sorry*

one time at a football game i drank
an iced peach tea with chewed up
dip in it and nobody told me

if ur gums are rotten that'd make
me happy. ~~im sorry~~

gums like burnt sardines.

—

and life keeps on screaming as i
drive from the back seat
and life keeps screeching as i howl
from the southeast
and life keeps shrieking as i scream
for it to mean.
  to say sorry

doom.

elucidation

courses are due

wager makes a fortune

emerald green frock

blinds like post malone teeth

entertain them in last days of disco

before the ocean

there is a pink painted door for

him,

jim the audience

the dating pool is small for women

who like men

we will all be fat soon

been so patient

will swallow a car soon

season a bus with nutritional yeast
and a vat of lard
soon
in the dark blush
pretended to rise clear off earth
instead of face this doom.

---

theta.

hunched over a bowl
of something i'm shoveling
spine not in good health

alpha.

staring down the barrel
should have screamed yes
future looks so bleak

zeta| gamma..

my legs tumble off
or maybe i wish them to
stinging needs to stop

heavy blood climbing
down my top stinging
please, it needs to stop

sigma.

in love is the only thing that means
why are people so green?
so stupid

epsilon.

large glass of sulfur
parasol strong support me
i am so dizzy

delta.

we are all one not
discerned, the equator
that burns our lips off

Subliminal Moped.

i wish you could be pretty without
having to watch what you eat
sugar free tangerine
sparkling water
soda streams

my mother acts like she hates
 "whoever raised me"

motorcycles are scary
but mopeds are cool
exhaust echoing,
the purr of the engine only for me.

i hate when ppl ask for pictures
it reminds me how much i hate
texting

time to eat crow

I'm not cut out for this work, it's
devouring my soul

here i am laughing
I shouldn't be

you mean the world to me
just thought you should know

girls are so strange when they find
out their boyfriends are gay

you would never find out if they
weren't ready to tell you by the
way
  they just might be waiting for you

and sometimes you sound like
subliminal music.
for this month, i've decided I'll ride
it
your subliminal moped.

 thankyou, you see me
and from my eyeline, you avail the
view

i'm a good little girl for you
 echoing: only for you ,
 only just for you.

Foodteeth.

This has turned out to be such a
drag.
i'm not picky ,
I get my knowledge from anyone
who can see.

He wears his energetic field on his
skin
 and it shines blue-purple

Would you lick the food off my
teeth
Do you really like me?

You should have played with me a
little first

pets and whispers to me
without breath

It makes you wonder
if there wasn't something to the
women in the ancient Village ,
worshiping the phallus of Shiva

as much as women are regarded as
art
and they are
it's just something
when you look at it :
marvelous ,
splendid ,
full of splendor ,
enchanting.

I don't think people Rave about it
enough
 but unlike stills of glamourous
women
 I would never be able to capture
the essence within one photo.
There is too much Hypno
in the movement.

Let me just have a moment with it
please
it's so pretty
just like a bedazzled baton

And when you conduct it
I sing like the philharmonic
instruments

I wonder if that means I failed as a
woman,
I'm supposed to be enchanting ♀
 But I guess
 like a little girl with the toy
 I'm entranced by you.

You're so mega.
regale us all with your tales of
boats and fly fishing.

If you leave now- everything we
had will be perfect forever.

For the rest of meaningful time.
I'm living an ultralife.

I see your face in all these places
but it's just shadows occupying
empty spaces

 I've written about you too much
I'll have to give you another name
 pretend you're someone else

I don't want to but I feel people are
getting annoyed
And I need enough money to move

And now when I picture you
you're out on the boardwalk
cuz you like beaches don't you?

Over Exuberant but it worked
Now I know you rrly did like me
 in hindsight- I see ,

you rrly liked me. My-

---

eta.

large glass of sulfur
parasol large to shade me
not used to the sun

tau.

pickles with peanut butter
sour and salty
my teeth need to be cleaned
 but the yellow reminds me how
much fun it is to eat.

sweaty sheets with your socks still
on
you should probably take them off
in the shower
but they remind u how happy u
are when you're
inside me.

rho.

sometimes
the only thing i can remember
anybody doing is not listening to
me.

the only thing i want to do
 is
not do anything.

just think and
 eat and look striking and
maybe sit in the shower and watch
the water roll off of u.

wondering what you do with ur
time when i'm not glued to u
all ur special thoughts i'd pay a
dime to see

all the things you've known that
would be unhelpful to me

take it by the neck and choke it
take it by the shaft and softly
stroke it
it's so pretty .

just like a bedazzled baton.

pi.

Soft feet outside the door

Me on the bathroom floor with

nailpolish drying

eta.

im going in the forest to lie beneath
the grass.
the idea of it verses it. it's different.

omicron.

i'm burning or made of fire
yearning is all, it raised me.

i am liionhearted but my hands
still shake
and my voice
 still
quakes
under the sound of stout men
walking outside my world

but not u
u have soft feet.

xi.

the stream rolls off of u
and splashes me
im alive
thanks for reminding me.

SLOWLY.

used sewing machine near me
preferably pale green
vintage vogue sewing patterns of
lingerie-
rainbow flower patterned panties
i'm concentrating, needle between
my teeth
 i don't want to mess them up.
the time goes by so slowly.

---

britney.

there are no psychedelics in my
head
just soft pretty thoughts
but i like the theatrics
so i rot in front of the television

the true savior of that film were the
two britney spears lyrics
and they knew it…
you could tell

i'm due west says the compass
with my soul falling over my head
sailing into navy on a marron ship

fueled by nail polish fumes and
nitrous

in the darkness all cats are grey
in the light the cats will play
what's the point of a 7/11 if it's not
open 24/7?
eating sunscreen, the only thing of
which has no end.

it will all blow over and if it
doesn't it still will
dust returns to dust and this is
how i rust
with my soul falling over my head
i can't swim with u if you're not
dead

"only the dead fish follow the
stream"-
whispers from the russian doll
bought from the mall in my
dreams
the gods kill the ones they love
when we're ready to be free
 (*the gods fill the ones they love when we're
ready to be free*)
the nice, the good, the sacred
machine
keeps on churning

the
pretty
priest
with the blue raspberry slurpee
that he almost didn't get

because what kind of gas station
closes?
says a eulogy for me

i hope they play *everytime* by
britney.
~~hey, heaven tastes just like broccoli.~~

greek key friese.

i enjoy being cryptic
where no one can understand me
because at least then there is a
reason
people don't listen

i'm done overexplaining,
no one cares to get it -
only me
cryptic

i think i am better than u,
only because i can feel what's in
my stomach
can't you hear it?

why won't you hear it?
it's like a god - we all have a god in
our stomachs.

---

nu.

words strike at midnight
haven't touched this in a long time
it's never too late for singing
there was this arena the talent
show
i didn't win it
i don't understand it
i sang happiness is a butterfly.

snow-skull.

soul tumbles past skull
sixty-eight and twenty-two
surrounded by clear
    free

mu.

snow powder and im an angel
grey skies and im a jet
may showers and i understand rain
the spring flowers do not need to
be ripped from their ground.

beta.

no one seems to realize
when they get closer and closer to
the old man,
until they are walking with him
and he lives in a garden.

lambda.

being in the moment
we can't plan life
when we surrender we're the most
alive

U are both of U,
    and the sea
Eternal Light.
…